Boundless Treasury of Blessings

A Collection of Prayers, Teachings and Poems

———

By Her Eminence
Jetsunma Ahkön Norbu Lhamo

Wild Dakini LLC
P.O. Box 304
Poolesville, Maryland 20837 USA

Copyright © Jetsunma Ahkön Norbu Lhamo 2018

All rights reserved. No part of this book may be reproduced in any form electronic or otherwise, without written permission from Jetsunma Ahkön Norbu Lhamo.

For more information on Jetsunma's books, poetry, lyrics and music go to www.tibetanbuddhistaltar.org

First edition

Printed in USA.

ISBN 978-0-9855245-5-5
Ebook ISBN 978-0-9855245-6-2
1. Spirituality 2. Buddhism 3. Poetry

Library of Congress Control Number 2018907104

Cover photo © Mannie Garcia

Content

- 5 Foreword
- 8 Acknowledgements
- 12 Awakening
- 15 Prayer to Compassionate Buddha I
- 17 Prayer to Compassionate Buddha II
- 19 24-Hour Prayer Vigil
- 21 The Caretakers Vow
- 23 Here is a teaching you did not ask for
- 25 The Wish-Fulfilling Jewel, A Practice of Devotion
- 29 Bodhisattva Vow
- 31 Renunciate Vows for Lay Practitioners
- 32 Invocation
- 34 Cry
- 39 Song to Tara
- 40 Prayer made at Amitabha Stupa in 1995
- 43 Samsara
- 50 Sang Wisdom
- 53 Prayer of Dedication to the Long Life of Ani Aileen
- 54 Shining Lake of Crystal Tears: A Confessional Prayer
- 57 Father
- 58 This Journey
- 59 The Feast
- 61 Tsawai Lama I
- 62 Tsawai Lama II
- 63 Better Listen!

- 65 Amitabha Practice Commentary given on Twitter
- 66 The Amitabha Practice
- 69 Series of Tweets
- 71 Young Throne Holder
- 73 The Heart Stream of Bodhicitta
- 75 From a series of tweets while at Palyul Ling Retreat Center in Upstate New York
- 77 Dedication Prayer for Palyul and Kunzang Ödsal Palyul Changchub Chöling
- 78 Dedication of Merit
- 80 Images
- 82 Glossary
- 87 About Jetsunma Ahkön Norbu Lhamo

Foreword

NAMO GURU DEWA DAKI YE

It is a great blessing and honor to have an opportunity to give a short introduction about Her Eminence Jetsunma Ahkön Norbu Lhamo and her noble activities.

Her Eminence Jetsunma Ahkön Norbu Lhamo is a Western reincarnation of a Bodhisattva who practices Secret Mantrayana and is spreading the Buddha's doctrine in the West in a way that is accessible to Westerners. I have known her since 1996, when His Holiness Pema Norbu Rinpoche enthroned her at Namdroling Monastery in Bylakuppe, India. She is the founder of Kunzang Ödsal Palyul Changchub Chöling (KPC), which is located in Poolesville, MD, USA. In this Dharma center, there is 24/7 prayer, group practice, recitation, and other spiritual and community activities; and it is open for the public as well.

In order to understand who Jetsunma is and what KPC is we must know a brief historical introduction to Buddhism and Tibetan Buddhism. The founder of Buddhism, Buddha Shakyamuni was born in Lumbini grove in Nepal, the son of King Sudhodana and Queen Maya Devi. His early life was spent in palatial luxury, and he excelled in all the pursuits of his time, both academic and athletic. Slowly he began to doubt the validity of his worldly life. At the age of 29, he renounced his worldly life, and left the palace. After six years of unwavering meditation, at the age of 35, he attained enlightenment.

Through his infinite compassion, Buddha started to teach, but his teaching was so vast and profound that it was broadly divided into three categories or levels which are now known as the Hinayana School, Mahayana School, and the Vajrayana or Secret Mantrayana School, which uses a variety of skillful methods to bring about that same vast and profound realization in a relatively short time. These different traditions were gradually propagated all over India, Nepal, and many other Asian countries. The Buddha's teachings are still unbroken today.

The Hinayana teachings have been preserved in Sri Lanka, Thailand, Cambodia and other countries in Southeast Asia. The Mahayana teachings have been preserved in China, Japan, and Korea; and the Vajrayana teachings have been preserved mainly in Tibet, Bhutan, and the Himalayan part of Nepal.

Tibet was doubly fortunate. Not only was it one of the few countries in which Vajrayana continued to be practiced, it was also the only one in which the full range of teaching, from all three traditions, was transmitted and preserved.

Over the centuries these many strands of the Buddha's teaching have been handed down from master to students, as demonstrated by the lineage holder. Today there are four main schools of Tibetan Buddhism. Of these four main schools, the Nyingma school was the very first Buddhist school in Tibet. It was established around the eighth century and is known as the old-translation school. The Kagyu, Shakya, and Gelug schools came after the tenth century and are called new-translation schools.

The first Nyingma school masters were mainly the Indian masters Shantarakshita, Vimalamitra and Padmasambhava, whom the Tibetans refer to as Guru Rinpoche, the precious Master. These masters handed down mainly the sutra and tantra teachings through fully realized Tibetan masters such as Longchen, Jigme Lingpa, Mipham Rinpoche and others. Within the Nyingma lineage, there are also six mother monasteries: Palyul, Kathog, Shechen, Dzogchen, Mindroling, and Dorje Drag.

Palyul was founded by Rigdzin Kunzang Sherab, the elder brother of the previous Ahkön Lhamo. The lineage was passed down from Rigdzin Kunzang Sherab to Pema Lhundrup Gyatso and Drubwang Pema Norbu Rinpoche through twelve Palyul lineage holders, to His Holiness Karma Kuchen Rinpoche and Her Eminence Jetsunma Ahkön Norbu Lhamo. All the teachings have been passed down unbroken from master to students until the present master.

Her Eminence Jetsunma Ahkön Norbu Lhamo is none other than an emanation of the great yogini Mandarava who was the consort of Guru Padmasambhava.

Jetsunma Ahkön Norbu Lhamo is a Bodhisattva who has boundless love and compassion toward all sentient beings. A Bodhisattva is one who has Bodhichitta (the mind of enlightenment), one who has transcended samsara. To be a genuine Buddhist practitioner, you must go through a traditional system. First, you must take refuge in front of the Three Jewels, the Buddha, Dharma, and Sangha, and also, in Vajrayana, in front of the root master (the guru). After that we also need to arouse the Bodhichitta. Without Bodhichitta we cannot possibly attain the ultimate goal of complete enlightenment. Then in the path of Dzogchen, Bodhicitta must be aroused because it is the only doorway to Dzogchen. In essence, all Dzogchen practice is guru yoga practice. It is a special, powerful, skillful means for accomplishing this path and attaining the siddhis, spiritual accomplishments. Just practicing only guru yoga will directly destroy dualistic thoughts. Then one can rest in the unaltered natural state of awareness (rigpa) itself.

I think Western people are very good at analyzing and researching the reason to practice, but in order to accomplish the practice itself, one must have a good master who can show the methods of skillful means and confer blessings. That could be the reason that the Bodhisattva, Jetsunma Ahkön Norbu Lhamo, came in Western form to teach Western people in their own language.

I wish and pray that this book will bring immense benefit to all the Western people as well as whoever sees it, reads it, contemplates it, and meditates on it. May all sentient beings be free from the ocean of suffering. May all sentient beings attain complete enlightenment in this very life.

May Bodhichitta, precious and sublime,
Arise where it has not yet come to be;
And where it has arisen may it never fail
But grow and flourish ever more and more.

— **Khenpo Pem Tsheri Sherpa**
  Namdröling Monastery

Acknowledgements

It took many devoted hearts and skills to create this book which could not have happened without the blessing of the compassion and wisdom of Jetsunma Ahkön Norbu Lhamo's presence in the world.

With gratitude, we acknowledge those who are responsible for making this book possible. The Boundless Treasury of Blessings is the inspiration of Michelle Adams. From her devotion and faith comes this treasury of Jetsunma's expressions of compassion and wisdom, with Michelle's trust that all who see them will benefit. The words have been complemented with photos of Jetsunma, His Holiness Penor Rinpoche and His Holiness Karma Kuchen Rinpoche as well as of sacred images. Thank you, Angela Adams, for putting it all together. The two of you have created a book that will inspire whoever has the good fortune to make a connection through its pages.

We also wish to thank Ani Atara Heiss for her effort preparing the book for publication, attending to the finer points that others of us are inclined to miss. To the many who provided photos and graphics: Mannie Garcia, Ted Kurkowski, Ani Aileen Williams, Ani Dawa Dellamulla, Ani Sonam Schroeder, Wib Middleton, John Buhmeyer and Ashby North. And thanks to KPC Palyul Archives for so willingly sharing from its own treasure chest.

With gratitude also to editorial staff, Ani Rinchen Khandro, Ani Tenzin Wangmo, Michelle Adams, and Michael Brunk. And to Ani Megan Gilana for her enthusiasm about getting Jetsunma's teachings out to the world.

The teachings of the Buddha have come to the West in many languages from many cultures. Jetsunma Ahkön Norbu Lhamo began teaching Buddhism in Maryland in 1982 before Buddhism was well known in America. Her teachings have always been pure, uncomplicated windows into the nature of mind, coming directly from her own experience. Although she referred to Buddha in early teachings, her language reflected the understanding of those who heard her. Until 1985, Jetsunma had never read a book on Buddhism. Then His Holiness Pema Norbu Rinpoche visited and told her she was teaching pure Mahayana Buddhism because she had done so many times in the past. Soon after that he officially recognized her as a tulku, the incarnation of the sister of the founder of his Palyul lineage.

In this book, you will see page after page of Jetsunma's presentations of the Buddha's teachings in prose and poetry, in song and in practices designed for Western students. Since Jetsunma began teaching over 35 years ago, she has made Buddhism meaningful in the English language in a way that is compatible with and accessible to Western culture. The words are an expression of the very fabric of her being. Jetsunma is here to teach, to guide, and to inspire us to discover our Buddha nature—the universal truth—to live in accordance with that truth, and to help others in whatever way we can.

Jetsunma met His Holiness Penor Rinpoche for the first time in 1985 during his visit to the United States. Penor Rinpoche, His Holiness Dilgo Khyentse Rinpoche, and Dzongnang Rinpoche agreed that Alyce Zeoli was indeed the reincarnation of Genyenma Akhön Lhamo, the sister of Rigdzin Kunzang Sherab, the First Throneholder of the Palyul lineage.

In 1988, His Holiness Penor Rinpoche traveled to Jetsunma's center in Poolesville, MD, which he named Kunzang Ödsal Palyul Changchub Chöling (KPC) and enthroned her as Jetsunma Ahkön Norbu Lhamo. Her recognition and enthronement marked the first time ever that a Western woman had been so recognized.

In 1994, His Holiness Kusum Lingpa, a Nyingma master and terton, further recognized Jetsunma as Princess Lhacham Mandarava, the Indian consort of Padmasambhava. In 2004, His Holiness Ngawang Tenzin, at the time the Dorje Lopon, or chief religious official, of Bhutan, reiterated this identification with Mandarava.

Awakening

I am Love,
I pour myself out
    on the waters…
      And the Earth.
Over time and space
I pour, I am,
    never ending.
I encompass all
    unto Myself.
I am pregnant with
    Creation.
I penetrate all.
I am fulfilled…
    Love.

I am Light.
The Light of the One…
    Of the All.
Radiant, life-giving,
I am…
      To BE.
I declare my Self
    In all things
And it is so.
I find my Self
    in Creation
and bear my Self
      forth
triumphant!
And all is perfect
because I am
    Light.

I am Spirit.
I am the song and the
    Breath
of the Infinite.
The sound and essence
    of the most subtle
        One.
I bring to you your birthright
    on silent, soaring
        wings.

Behold, I come quickly.

Look within.
    I am here.
I speak to you,
    from deep within you.
And now you hear me.
You let me heal you.
You let me radiate from you
You let me claim you as
    My own.

Let us make a pact,
You, who I am.
To know our oneness.
To renounce duality.
To know only Truth.
For I speak to you
    Even as you call
        To Me.
"Awaken… Awaken…
    This is the beginning."

1984

Prayer To Compassionate Buddha I

Lord Buddha, Buddha of Compassion,
Plant in my heart the seed of love,
Plant in the deepest part of me
The Light of Compassion.
Take from me all self absorption.
Teach me to give myself over to Love.

Lord Buddha, do with me what is thy will.
Whether I am sad or human or angry.
Take from me all parts of myself.
Remove from me all obstacles for I have one purpose
    and one purpose only:
that where I am You might be;
that through me the Buddha of Compassion
    might come to the world.
I prostrate myself completely.
Let there be no self—only compassion.
Where I am let Love live.

1984

Prayer To Compassionate Buddha II

In all the universe there is One Life.
One Life most precious, come from the Void, from the
    stillness, from the fullness, from the Absoluteness.
It is a Life never ending.
It is the Cosmic Buddha.
In all the universe, there is One Life.
It is that One.

Most precious Buddha, I live for you and I would die for you.
For that which is called "I" is only apparent.
You are the Truth, the Hope, and the Holiness.
Absorb me back into yourself.
Allow me to enter again into that holy place where in all
    the universe there is One Life.
And as this truth reflects like a diamond in all directions, so,
    Lord Buddha, where I am let there be nothing but a clear place
    by which your Grace, your Compassion, your Light, the Life that is
    true, might enter the world.

Make of me a clean thing, a pure thing, that when I look
    upon myself, I see that One Life, most precious,
    that where I am, your hand, your face, your heart are
    available to all sentient beings.

What is my life, what are my thoughts, what are my
    distractions, when in their stead you might be here?
Remove from me all obstacles to that perfection.
Do with me whatever is necessary that I might lie down in
    peace and you might rise up.

Whatever tiny things I have done that were good, in the face
    of your glory, they are nothing.

Lord Buddha, where I am now, may you be, always
and for all time, forever and eternally until all sentient
    beings are free.
Take this place that I offer and come into the world.

For the sins I have committed with my body, speech and
    mind, forgive me.
Remove all obstacles.
I give you permission.
Do with me whatever is necessary that absolute purity
    be attained.
Not even that Buddhahood should be realized, but only
    absolute purity, so that Buddhahood can even
    be conceived.

Make of me a clean place that where I am all sentient
    beings may have food and drink, that they can enter
    into me and be healed, that I can enter them and live.
Where I am, let the Buddha of Compassion come to
    the earth.
And let it be now.

Lord Buddha, take me home.
Make of me a clear place.
Help me to lie down so that you might rise and show
    your glory to all sentient beings.
Let it always be so until they are all at peace.
Take this place that I offer and come into the world.
So be it.

1984

24-Hour Prayer Vigil

On April 18, 1985, Jetsunma and her students made a commitment to begin Prayer Without Ceasing until there was no more suffering. Since then the 24 hour prayer vigil for world peace has continued unbroken at the temple in Poolesville, Maryland. On February 2015, the KPC California center began a Prayer Vigil which is ongoing without interruption for 12 hours each Wednesday. It is Jetsunma's wish that one day there will be prayer vigils occurring around the world.

Prayer Vigil participants take two hour shifts, making prayers and chanting mantra dedicated to the benefit of all beings. Kind-hearted and selfless motivation is the root, the foundation of the prayer vigil.

The Caretakers Vow

We, the Caretakers of the Earth, dedicate ourselves to the liberation and salvation of all sentient beings. We vow to work for the liberation of planet Earth from the clutches of suffering, poverty, famine and death. We vow to return in whatever form necessary, under whatever necessary conditions, so that all Earth creatures can be liberated from the ravages of cyclic existence.

We vow to work for world peace. We vow to work for the raising of all the nations of Earth into a state of union and ultimately into the blessed state of supreme wisdom, the wisdom that is beyond all description. We vow to work toward a great Universal Quickening of mind and heart, leading all beings to a state of clarity, a state in which Chenrezig, the Buddha of Compassion, is enthroned within all hearts and within the planetary heart.

We vow to offer as food and drink to all sentient beings the clear, sweet Dharma so that they may feast and be satisfied at last. We offer our bodies, our speech, and our minds to be filled like bowls with Dharma that in our joy we will spill over into the waiting hearts of all our brethren. May their suffering cease forever.

To all the blessed Tathagatas, to all the root Lamas, to all the Sangha, to all the caretakers, grant us the strength to continue, the clarity to overcome self-cherishing, the determination to return forever until we are the last, and finally, the grace to find our way home. May the Dharma take root in the West, on the Earth, and in the hearts of all sentient beings. So be it.

The merit of the dedication of these vows and of the building of this place of practice is offered.

To our root Lamas: His Holiness Padma Norbu Rinpoche, Ven. Gyatrul Rinpoche
To our spiritual friends: Ven. Khenpo Palden Sherab Rinpoche, Ven. Khenpo Tsewang Dongyal Rinpoche, and to His Holiness Dudjom Rinpoche. And to all parent sentient beings who have gifted us with fire in our hearts and light on our way.

I take refuge in the Lama.
I take refuge in the Buddha.
I take refuge in the Dharma.
I take refuge in the Sangha
With all beings equal to space.

August 31, 1986

Here is a teaching you did not ask for:

Try to believe in the Love….that the Love that exists is Absolute. It never varies, it is unchanging. You did nothing to deserve it and you cannot destroy it. It is your belief in the Love, your acceptance of it, this changes from moment to moment, circumstance to circumstance, tossed about on the waves of your emotions.

Let your heart fall deeper under the surface to where the waves seem very far away. There you will find it, and me. Make a samaya now to go deeper every day, to diligently travel to that calm place where the sands do not shift at all.

You never asked for this! Only for what is temporary, turbulent, based on a self that you have only imagined. Learn to ask for what is true. That you will be answered is certain because the answer is already accomplished.
Beneath the waves it is already there.

I am with you again, still, always.

I do love you.

Written as a birthday gift for her student, Elizabeth Elgin,
September 20, 1986 in Poolesville, Maryland.
May all who read this teaching know it is for them.

The Wish-Fulfilling Jewel
A Practice of Devotion

First, visualize your Lama, not in personality, but as radiant clear light. You must visualize that all the external things such as facial features and clothing and the like are replaced by clear light. Visualize that well.

Then you must visualize within that form the heart of the Lama. See it as radiant, and you may picture its position as the same as the heart chakra, marked by an open lotus.

Next, you rejoice that your Lama's heart is open to you and that you may partake and enter and be at home. Rejoice that infinite love is there, that infinite Buddha is there also, and—this is important—that your Lama has come back for you.

Next you are to visualize and see, and understand, that all the hearts of every Buddha, all the enlightened sangha, are there, resting upon that lotus. If it helps, you may visualize a radiant Buddha on top of that lotus. Know, though, in your deepest heart, that all the Buddhas rest there.

Then, see yourself as radiant light as well, all the ego washed away, all the rigidity is gone. And now, take your heart, whatever condition it is in, open or closed, afraid or not, saddened or burdened or joyful—and merge it with the heart of the Lama until they are one heart. You have both entered into the heart of the Lama and received the Lama into your own heart. Now, with great joy, look within and see that all the Buddhas now live within you.

This practice should be done every day at least once, but always first thing in the morning. That is significant; it must be first thing in the morning. At the end of your practice, with great joy and a spirit of giving, imagine within you what gifts you can give your Lama this day. Will it be that this day, through the gift of the heart of the Buddhas you will destroy all negative thought? Or will it be that this day you will love truly unconditionally? Will it be that you will practice with a great diligence the Bodhisattva vows during all that you do?

What gifts will you give your Lama this day? It must be a gift of spirit and you must never tell another. This is between you and your Lama. It will be seen and known and recognized.

Do you understand the practice and do you see its value? This is your first practice, quite a valuable one. It can serve to bring you forth into something else, new and glorious. It will give you great joy, the deepest and most profound pleasure. It will open your heart and cause it to be rid of so much samsara. As time goes on and more devotional practices are given, there will be specific techniques by which you can utilize the grace of your Lama's heart and its merging with yours as a vehicle for abolishing samsaric tendencies from your life. It is a true vehicle, not an imaginary one. This is not visualization. This is a true thing. Do you understand?

Once that relationship has been attained, you can count on it. It will support you and if you make a mistake, it will come back for you. It will help you attain all of your dreams, all of your hopes, and truly, it will help you attain your Bodhisattva vow.

It is an everlasting gift and a true relationship.

1986

Bodhisattva Vow

I dedicate myself to the liberation and salvation of all sentient beings.

I offer my body, speech, and mind in order to accomplish the purpose of all sentient beings.

I will return in whatever form necessary, under extraordinary circumstances to end suffering.

Let me be born in times unpredictable, in places unknown, until all sentient beings are liberated from the cycle of death and rebirth.

Taking no thought for my comfort or safety, precious Lama (Buddha), make of me a pure and perfect instrument by which the end of suffering and death in all forms might be realized.

Let me achieve perfect enlightenment for the sake of all beings.

And then, by my hand and heart alone, may all beings achieve full enlightenment and perfect liberation.

1987

Renunciate Vows For Lay Practitioners

From this moment forward, I offer this life as a gift to the Three Precious Jewels.

My pure intention is to accomplish the purpose of self and others—Supreme Enlightenment—quickly and surely.

- Thus I vow that all my life, every portion, shall be used to accomplish that goal.
- All my activities shall accomplish that goal.
- All my thoughts and feelings are directed toward that goal.
- All my possessions shall be to strengthen and support that goal.
- I shall seek all appropriate teachings, empowerment and spiritual activities in order to secure that goal.
- My own enlightenment is now considered to be equal to and non-dual with the enlightenment of others.
- Therefore I vow to support fully, and without hesitation, the practicing spiritual community.
- I vow to support fully and with unconditional love the Three Precious Jewels and their manifestations: the Sangha and Temple.
- I will not kill.
- I will not lie to accomplish selfish purpose.
- I will not steal.
- I will not become intoxicated and thereby forget my purpose and vows.
- I will not engage in adultery or any promiscuous activity by which my intention will be compromised.
- I fully intend to do all I can to accomplish the liberation of all sentient beings and my own equally.
- I consider the realization of all beings to be equal with my own and of equal value.
- I fully support the spiritual community and its purpose on earth.
- Should any activity, possessions or relationship be contrary to these purposes, I will systematically change it or eliminate it from my life.

This I promise so that there will be an end to hatred, greed and ignorance within my mind stream and within the three thousand myriads of universes and so that myself and all beings will achieve precious awakening.

February 1987

Invocation

Lord Guru, teach me to see your face
Rinpoche, teach me to call your name
Come Come Come Come
Appear in Nirmanakaya form
Make your holy face appear
Be known to us now
Do not leave us comfortless
Do not abandon your vow
Bring us your nectar
For we thirst… We thirst!
And we cry to you
Stainless, Precious One!
Without your blessing we are helpless
Do not refuse this voice

I offer my body, speech and mind
Take this body to enhance your activity
Make of this speech a perfect voice
And in my mind you are enthroned
Upon the lotus in my heart

Use me Use me Use me
For the sake of all beings
That they might be free
Ah La La Ho
Ah La La Ho
Ah La La Ho
For their sake, my children
For their sake, my children

On April 2, 1992, Jetsunma Ahkön Lhamo spontaneously brought forth *Invocation*, a mystical message in the form of a chanted prayer that penetrates to the very core of the listener. Recognizing the special nature of *Invocation*, it was decided to professionally produce a studio recording. This CD features the 18-minute recording that followed, faithfully capturing the same essence of that first live expression.

Essentially, *Invocation* is an expression of longing for true wisdom and compassion to make its appearance in the world and liberate beings from their confusion and suffering. This expression has three parts. The first conveys unwavering insistence that the pure teacher appear to bring direct blessing to those who have no means to comprehend and eradicate the root of their suffering. The second part is total compassionate surrender, the offering of one's own body, speech and mind as the means by which these blessings might reach others. The third section expresses the vow to continue to accomplish the purpose of these blessings until such time as all beings without exception are freed from the endless cycle of death and rebirth.

Invocation can be used as a profound meditational practice as it naturally stimulates and calls forth compassion and devotion within the mind. It has been formally recognized as a proper method of practice by His Holiness Penor Rinpoche, the supreme head of the Nyingma Tradition of Tibetan Buddhism at that time. For the best results, sit comfortably with the spine straight. Quietly engage in the motivation or wish to be of benefit to oneself and others equally, and then listen as though you are pronouncing the words yourself, invoking pure mind, the mind of Enlightenment, to be present. It is very beneficial to listen to *Invocation* for an extended length of time with complete absorption allowing the mind to relax into its natural state. CD players with a continuous play function are helpful in this regard. This form of meditation is considered to be an act of virtue if done with selfless intention and the strong wish to benefit others. Therefore, at the end of your meditation session, it is appropriate to dedicate one's efforts to the Awakening of all beings.

"To all who can hear the precious sounds and words of Dharma: Please listen again to this '*Invocation* to Guru Rinpoche.' Allow this special gift from Jetsunma Ahkön Lhamo to inspire the spontaneous increase in Bodhicitta (love and compassion) in your life. Always cultivate Bodhicitta. That is the purpose of your precious human life."

– His Holiness Penor Rinpoche

Cry

In our divided clinging consciousness
In our ego-centered dreaming
we are bound.
Flung, unaided,
Unable to distinguish
The nature that is peace.

Drunken
Imagining distinction
in the nature that
is form and formless

Grieving
For we have seen the difference
Between the crystal
And the nectar that fills it
with its emptiness

Oh..
If we could only taste
the soundless voice
that sings its silent name
In colors

OM
Vairocana, Holy Holy
Bring the blessed kindest
Wisdom of the Dharmadhatu
To this singer's song

Scream!
For we are angry
we are chained
In our self-righteousness
we are prisoners and wardens

Alone
No love in hate
No reason, no meaning
Hallucination, like a drug
we're burning

Stiff
with jaundiced principles
disjointed, numbed
We've sold our value
for a nightmare

Sick
and filled with venom
we are dead and dying
scratching at our eyes
that we might see

Locked
in form, in function
In making statements
meaningless in the silence
of our indivisibility

HUNG
Vajrasattva, Blessed Blessed
Bring the mirror wisdom
To the crying ones
who long to see your face

Running
In our race
to nowhere
Pumped with
self value
Our holy war

Straining
With increasing tension
Structuring conviction
Deny that I am you
can't see your eyes

Plumped
And filled with dirty
hard distinctions
We are successful
We have sat our
hellish throne

Preening
In the gorgeousness
of reason
Reasons not to give our lives
Oh, take this life

Truly
We try so hard
to know the rapture of union
Impossible to know
with hearts so dry

SO
Ratnasambhava, Buddha
Buddha
Bring the view
of equanimity
like holy wine
to this tired burning child
Need
The force is boundless
the aching endless
It never ceases
We are obsessed

Craving
The fire burns us
Our lips are parched
Our eyes, our hearts
Know no release

Pointless
The endless seeking
brings more of nothing
The suffering of suffering
has reached its peak

Moving..this restless
searching
I think of babies
crying
for the mother's breast

Touch us
We need to feel it
It all seems
out there
Beyond our reach

AH
Amitabha, Purest Pure One
Cleanse our Perception
Bring the feast
of Pure Discrimination
to our hungry mouths

Wounded
Worlds of wounded
Crying and helpless
No one to hear them
Too much jealousy and fear

Wasted
Too tired and jaded
Sick and faded
Certain of my fix,
my gig, my sphere

Unaided
Standing alone in
mute acceptance
Burden of proof
so heartless
That we are here

We are
I am
Engaged
In righteous battle
I am unique!
Distinguished!
Endless is my work!

Please
There must be something
Or maybe someone
Responding sweetly
But never me
For I cannot

HA
Amoghasiddhi, Sublime
Dancer
Bring us the movement
The sweet activity
Of Perfect Love

1992

Song To Tara

Clear Mind
Holy Mind
The arguments we have used against you
are like dust...
Against You?
You, who flow silently...
eternally in the well of our hearts.

Have we robed you in filthy rags
Hatred....greed....ignorance?
You have remained steadfast, unchanging

Today we lift you up to the lips
and hearts of beings without number
And are feasted, forever.

Precious mind unchanging
Clear mind eternal.
The promise we have searched for is
enthroned in our hearts.

Clear light, holy light
Stainless, precious heart.
Here in this clear place we are robed in
sweet scent and victorious forever.

1992

Prayer made at Amitabha Stupa in 1995

Gathering together whatever virtue I have accumulated in the three times, this I offer to the Supreme Lama who is my only Refuge. Please, Lord Guru, care for me. Do not abandon me in samsara. Please help me transform my pitiful efforts into a perfect vehicle by which sentient beings will be liberated.

May Kunzang Palyul Chöling (KPC) be an ever increasing Light in these dark times. May it always be a place of pure practice, Dharma study, and compassionate activity. May KPC grow and expand quickly and in a stable way in order to meet the needs of all beings. In the coming times of darkness, may KPC provide refuge and spiritual nourishment, particularly the excellent teachings of Vajrayana Buddhism, and by that merit may it hold back the dark times. May KPC, from this time forward, attain affluence and prosperity, so that all bills will be paid, all debts resolved, and so that we will easily accomplish all projects.

May every practitioner here attain Supreme Enlightenment swiftly and surely. May these goals be accomplished by KPC:

> The Great Statue of Amitabha
> The Great Statue of Arya Tara
> A Hospice for Practitioners
> Retreat Centers
> A Shedra for Dharma Study
> A Children's School for all grades

May the outreach of KPC grow so that Dharma is available worldwide. May I open Temples and Dharma Centers throughout the nation and the world.

I pray for the strength and energy and courage necessary to accomplish all my obligations concerning sentient beings. May I never hesitate or lack in strength, power and courage, so that I can be of supreme benefit. I pray to the Guru that I will remain firm and strong and live love, to the age 108 for the sake of beings.

I pray for my family. May they practice Dharma purely and attain supreme realization. May they help to propagate Dharma for the sake of beings. May their lives be long and full and happy. May they meet their perfect mates and enjoy a long and perfect spiritual union.

May all my students be blessed. May those who are spiritually challenged turn fully to Dharma and be liberated. May those whose hearts are pure remain firm and filled with devotion and virtue and may they be liberated fully.

I pray for the end of all sufferings, such as: war, hunger, sickness, non-virtue, old age, death, mental confusion.

I pray for all children. May they have love, guidance and Dharma in their lives, plenty to eat and all comfort, including happiness. I pray for the KPC children; may all obstacles in their lives and practice be pacified.

May all students who have lost the path and broken their samaya be restored.

I pray for all animals; may they be liberated, as well as all realms be emptied.

May all obstacles to prosperity be removed swiftly in order that we may support Dharma projects.

May there be an end to all domestic violence, child abuse and alcoholism.

Lastly, for myself I pray. May I always return for sentient beings and increase in potency and swift action for their sake. May I not grow tired, weary, afraid, discouraged, weak, apathetic. Help me to overcome and be strong. May I prepare well for my next life so that I may be useful.

I dedicate this prayer to the long life of all pure Lamas, and most especially, I pray for the long life of His Holiness the Dalai Lama, His Holiness Penor Rinpoche, and the Venerable Gyatrul Rinpoche.

Samsara

Buddhas and Bodhisattvas, please listen to me!
From the depth of my heart I beg you to remain!
I offer all virtue I have accumulated in the three times.
Please accept for the sake of sentient beings.
I request you to remain in the world for the sake of the lost.
I request you to give instruction for the sake of the deluded.
Grant blessings for the sake of the poor and hungry.
Increase the strength of Dharma until none can resist!

Suppress with your splendor the horrors of hatred, greed
    and ignorance.
Do not abandon us!

This pitiful practitioner, this humble servant of the Three
Precious Jewels, this poor steward of lost beings begs
    you to hear these verses.

Please accept them as my timeless vow.
Please remind me in every future time of these words.
Please let me perform this duty in order to benefit beings,
    and so that in some small way I can repay the kindness
    of my Teachers.

To Guru Rinpoche, I pray.
Lord of my Three Doors
Do not abandon me.
I, your humble servant
Am concerned for sentient beings.
Here I am, to promise you
I have not forgotten my vows
Spoken before your Holy Face.
Again I lay them at your feet
For their sake.
As you have taught me.

Bitch,

I have seen you.
I have heard your voice.
I have smelt your smell.
I have lived
    and died with you.
I know your name . . .

Samsara.

Bitch, whore,
Whatever garment you wear
    I will know you.
Your smile is no seduction
    to me.

You will appear
    in lovely forms,
Seductive, caressing, singing songs
    filled with promises
It is then I will appear
    far more beautiful than you
Adorned with garments
    of pure aspiration
Resplendent with gold and gems
    of pure bliss.
From my mouth will come
    the ambrosia of Dharma
And from your
    grasping arms
I will steal my children away,
Like a thief
    in the night . . .
And lead them to
    Paradise.

Bitch

You will be known
    as mother
And from your teats
    my babies will suckle
    vomit and death.
You will cradle them in
    arms of deception
    and sorrow.
Saying "trust in me"
    "I am your mother"

Then I will appear
    vast as the sky
With arms that reach
    around the world.
From pure white breasts
    I will offer the milk
    of Bodhicitta.
My arms will reach into
    hell itself, to every place.
Joyfully I will hold my children
Saying "You, my darlings
    are sons and daughters
    of the Buddhas and Bodhisattvas"
Singing
    "You are the child of
    luminosity
    the Holy Display of the
    Sphere of Truth"
And then, offering sweets
    succulent and filled with
    Love
They will follow me
    and I will lead them
    to Paradise.

Whore.

You will appear as the demon.
Death, fear, hatred
    selfishness, greed, ignorance . . .

These will be your
    unholy teachings.
Ugly and terrifying, you will
    manipulate my children.
Like the helpless and blind,
They will follow any sound
    without distinction.
Then I will come
    I will be uglier than you
My yellow fangs will be
    terrible to see!
From my mouth will come
    an unbearable howl.
Fierce and dominating
    my voice will be heard
    above yours.
My feet will walk
    all the worlds
    all the realms.
My arms, with terrifying claws
    will reach into every corner.
I will clasp my children
    every one.
With great cries of suppression
I will tear them from you
    Hell-Bitch
And carry them to Paradise.

Be warned,
    Whore-mother of suffering
I am coming.
I am relentless!
Not one of my children
    will I abandon to you.
I will meet you on
    every hill and mountain.
In every ocean, in every country.
In the sky, in the six realms,
In form and formless lands,
No hell or heaven will
    hide you from me.
I will never stop.
Like a tigress
    I will come
Mouth dripping with blood,
Claws extended.

I will come and slay you,
I alone will defeat you.
I will rip you apart
Cut up, shredded,
    sliced and diced
No one will know
    which part to call Samsara.
I will finish you.
    You will not enslave my children.

Then I will shed tears
    to heal you.
I will scoop you up
    in my arms
Tenderly I will hold
    your head.
My eyes will shine
    wisdom and compassion upon you

My body will be your home.
My speech will sing lullabies
    of pure virtue.
Then you will remember
    you are my child, too.
Samsara.
    Yes, you too.
Then, beloved child
    who is never separate from me,
We will depart together.
We will be in Paradise.

Colophon:

Written by Jetsunma on February 16, 1996 when two of her beloved students were caught in terrible ignorance and delusion and could not see the face of the Guru. In an extreme and powerful display of wrathful compassion, she wrote this war cry to benefit all beings who are lost in samsara, with intention to offer these verses to Guru Rinpoche at Maritika Cave in Nepal during pilgrimage in March, 1996. After writing these verses, in her purity and compassion, she apologized to us, her powerless students, for not being more beautiful, or more fierce and ugly, in order that she would lead us out of suffering. Witnessing this miraculous display, I asked to type this prayer and made a vow to take this as my heart practice until samsara is emptied. May all who read this and hold it within their hearts know the Dakini, inseparable with the Guru, and never rest until all beings are free. Witnessed by her sons, Ben Zeoli and Rigdzin Zeoli, and myself, her pitiful attendant, Elizabeth Elgin; by this display may all beings be led to Paradise.

Sang Wisdom

Sang Wisdom
To the Fire
Warm me,
And he replied
Breathe, Beloved
For he knew
Her breath is fire, too.
So she did
And the cycle was
Complete.

Cried Wisdom
To the Fire
Carry me!
And he replied
Sing Beloved
For he knew
that the sound of ecstasy
was a song he had heard
and never forgotten
once, and very soon again.
So she did
And the nectar of love
filled the worlds.

Called Wisdom
to the Fire
I cannot see you,
come to me.
And he replied
Close your eyes, Beloved
For he knew
that Wisdom is innocent
of time and space.
So she did
And she remembered.

Thus, the magical empowerment
of the Divine Consorts
was born again
and filled the worlds.
The sweetness tasted again
Of what has always been
One.

November 1996

Prayer of Dedication to the Long Life of Ani Aileen

By the blissful union of Guru Padmasambhava
and Mandarava
By the blessing of their perfect purity
By the blessing of their compassionate intention;
Their union, purity, and compassion;
these three
By this living, untainted power,
even in dark times
May the life of Ani Thubten Chödron be made
strong and firm.

By the power of the Dakini Lacham Mandarava
to make the life of the Lama strong,
May Ani-la, all sentient beings and myself also
Have a long life adorned with the
accomplishment of pure Dharma.

January 27, 2000

This was witnessed by Ani Atara Eileen when Jetsunma removed obstacles to the life of Ani Thubten Chödron. May the merit of this miraculous prayer be dedicated to the strong health and long life of the Dakini, Jetsunma Ahkön Norbu Lhamo.

Shining Lake of Crystal Tears
A Confessional Prayer

Arya Tara, Noble One
We bow down to your Lotus Feet
And beg you to remain enthroned
On the Lotus Throne within our hearts.

We your daughters and sons
Offer you the essence of whatever purity we may possess in the three times.
Please accept the nectar of our pitiful practice
Please bless the potential of all our hopes and aspirations
And guide our lips and blind eyes

To suckle at the breasts of the Sublime Bodhicitta.

Mother Tara, protect us, now and at the time of death
Soothe and cleanse our minds of the sickness and
fever of worthless distractions.
Hear us, Holy One, even though our very voices are
tainted with fear and slothfulness, weakened by
samsara's spell.

Oh Mother, when we have caused you sorrow
How will you then appear for us in Nirmanakaya form
Through endless eons for our sake-
How, Mother, will this occur
When our hearts and minds turn inward
With darkness and lack of caring for the suffering of
others?

Oh Mother Tara, Holy One, Perfect One
We are lost.
Now more than ever darkness comes
And we are overcome with our weakness and
poor view.

Yet You remain for us.

Blessed Mother, Holy One, this very day
We make our hearts and minds your home
We beg you to come in glory
and to remain with us.
With your Supreme Beauty, Sublime Power
and Faultless Light
Until we are inseparable
And samsara is emptied.

Composed August 24, 2004 in Sedona, Arizona after an ordained member
fell under samsara's dark spell.

Photo: © Mannie Garcia

Father

Lord of my life, sweet holy light
It's you that claimed me
It's you that saved me
It's you that I follow, always
'Till suffering ends
'Till it ends

Om Ah Hung Benzar Guru Pema Siddhi Hung

An excerpt from the lyrics of "Father"

This Journey

The Journey
From the birth of yearning
To the moment of recognition
The path, this journey, is method.
One's true nature the precious seed—
Buddha ground.
One's journey, this path—the method.
The awakening—this fruit—the treasure.
How astonishing!
The ground, the path, the fruit are Buddha.
Praise to the Nirmanakaya Buddhas who walk the earth!
Praise to the sons and daughters who follow them!
May I myself return again and again for them.
May I never grow weary, or bored of helping them.
May I nurture, teach, and feed them precious fruit.
May I never abandon the supreme samaya!

October 21, 2009

The Feast

The banquet is ready
The feast is set
And never will I forget
The taste, the sweetness.
The Bodhicitta, sublime display
Of all the Buddhas. Sweetness
Without measure. Peerless pleasure
The dazzling play of light
And essence.
Oh! For the day still coming
When virtue prevails
The ship to Liberation sails
For you. Come aboard!
Know the Lotus Lord.
In this day, in this time,
Taste the bliss—love sublime awaits.
Where are you? Will you obey
The call within, or turn away?
Will the treasure be yours, today?
Oh, Beloved, will you stay?

October 23, 2009

Tsawai Lama I

The colors of Autumn in full measure
Bring to mind the ultimate pleasure
A great Mandala, an offering treasure
I offer to the Guru, gone beyond.
If my eyes know beauty, it is His.
If the scent is sweet, it is His.
If the sound is lovely, it is His.
If the breeze is silk, it is His.
He who brought to me in this life
The ancient wisdom again, that Light.
The root of accomplishment, that One.
Only He warms my heart like the sun.
He will come again in glory
To sing His precious, ancient story.
Never mind the time of tears.
I cannot doubt that He is here.

October 25, 2009

Tsawai Lama II

It's raining now, but I can see
That soon the sun will be with me.
It's pouring now, but I can tell
That soon the bliss will come, as well.
That kiss of sunlight, a warming spell
Reminds me that when darkness fell
It seemed I'd lost you for a while
But then the gift—your blessing smile.
I knew that it would take some time
That soon the glory that is your Mind
Will come again, and in a while
You will come as a precious child.
Oh, lead me swiftly to that day
When I can close my eyes and pray
When I will know in that secret way
He has come! He is here! The great display!

October 27, 2009

Better Listen!

Crazy Wisdom lives inside my head.
Holy dreams when I go to bed
Bitter tears that I cannot shed
Ya better listen.
So much suffering that we cannot see
That's the way it will always be.
Until you yourself set your mind free
Ya gotta listen.
When your only dream is about yourself
And your heart so cold you love no one else.
Will you die this way? Or ask for help?
Ya better listen.
I know only love is worth our time.
Will we reach our bliss with a life sublime
Or just continue to run blind?
Ya gotta listen!

November 5, 2009

Amitabha Practice Commentary given on Twitter

I'd like to address the very newest Dharma practitioners, and offer the #METHOD I speak so often and so fondly of. All can benefit. Many are interested in Buddhism, read and think about it, enjoy it's thoughtfulness. But the main point of Dharma is accomplishment.

One can be a friend of Dharma, a supporter, collector, even a Guru junkie! But the point of Dharma is awakening, and method applied.

There are no quick and easy routes, no magic buttons, no gadgets, no tincture of this or that worth the money or effort. Dharma is free.

All you really need is a comfy cushion, a quiet sacred space, a mala (prayer beads), an image relating to your practice really helps.

Most practice requires empowerment (wang), breath transmission (lung), and the Lama's commentary. Therefore one needs a qualified Guru.

Fortunately, through compassion, certain Buddhas have made themselves more accessible in these times. One is Buddha Amitabha. Amitabha vowed that anyone speaking His mantra or even hearing it, He would liberate at death, thus accomplishing Dharma in one life.

Practicing Amitabha, then, is swift and extraordinary, can be done without wang or lung if the strong vow is made to seek these out asap.

As quickly as possible these tweets will be arranged usefully with an image of Amitabha for practice. Now, settle onto your cushion.

Allow the mind to simply relax and clear. Practice makes perfect, you will improve in time. The body is relaxed but the spine straight, the legs should be crossed Indian style or lotus style, but comfortable.

2009

The Amitabha Practice

Instantly in the space in front and above arises Buddha Amitabha. He is red in color with one face and two hands resting in His lap, palms up with knuckles touching. This mudra symbolizes meditative equipoise. He is holding a begging bowl and wearing robes of ordination, seated in lotus posture. He is surrounded with His retinue of sublime ones.

As we are awed by His splendor, we take refuge with body, speech, and mind: **"Buddha Amitabha I take refuge in you in this and every life"** (repeat three times).

Then, thinking kindly of all sentient beings, recite: **"For the sake of beings I give rise to the Bodhicitta so all may benefit"** (repeat three times). If you have a pure Lama, consider that while the appearance is Amitabha, the essence is identical to one's Root Guru. If not, get one.

Then hold the mala and recite the mantra, **OM AMI DEWA HRI**, counting one full mala which is 108 repetitions.

While reciting, one concentrates on compassion as motivation, the extraordinary qualities of Amitabha, the yearning for liberation in one life.

So the mind should be filled with pure devotion and wholesome yearning, and kindness toward all beings, every one, animals, ALL.

After at least one full mala of mantra, recite:

"I prostrate to Amitabha Buddha!"
"May I be reborn in the pure realm of great bliss."

Then Amitabha and his entourage dissolve into light, and pour into the top of one's head (crown), which mixes like milk and water with one's mind.

"And may all sentient beings without exception be placed in that very state."
This is a VERY condensed method, taken from Nam Chö.

The best thing to do is make a commitment to do this practice every day. It is in the commitment and the doing that benefits, along with the very sacred mantra and the blessing it holds. Therein lies benefit and accomplishment. Samaya.

Series of Tweets

Mother Goddess Earth, holy mother Tara, grant the blessing that I may have help and strength to provide for your babies, and grant blessings that I may give this little broken place back to you, whole and healed. KYE HO!

Hear this cry and accept these tears from a Dakini who is your daughter, your servant and your lover. May you recover, and may those who see "The Way" join hands as one people. Let us pay it forward. Eh Ma Ho!

OM MANI PEDME HUNG! OM TARE TUTTARE TURE SOHA!

I have to know, and truly feel we should pay attention! It is our planet, our Mother. We must hold her in our collective arms and hearts so she can heal. This is possible only if we all work together.

Our Earth—her winds are our breath, her water our blood, her ground our skin, her mountains and rocks our bones—she is heart of our hearts, flesh of our flesh, the Mother, our protectoress, now she cries out for help and we must not let her come to harm. We are inseparable from her, she from us.

Human kind must learn this lesson at last. Hear her call! Wake up! There is so little time.

Note: Her Eminence, Jetsunma Ahkön Norbu Lhamo, has given many Teachings about caring for our planet, Mother Earth. After the Fukushima, Japan, earthquake, Jetsunma gave a series of teachings on Twitter, asking every religion and nation to join in prayer to help our precious planet. All of the teachings can be found on her blog, TibetanBuddhistAltar.org.

March–April 2011

Photo: © Mannie Garcia

Young Throne Holder

Prince of power this is the hour
This is the time when you must shine
I see it on your face, in your mind
You awaken right on time
To honor our Guru, our Lord Sublime.

You alone are well prepared
This time would come, you were aware
He gave you his essence with such care
I would have known Him anywhere.
You mixed your minds like water and wine

I hear His song in your mind.

Composed August 25, 2011, during HH Karma Kuchen's visit to Kunzang Palyul Chöling

The Heart Stream of Bodhicitta

AH—May all beings be free of suffering.

May they recognize what to accept and what to reject, and pacify the root causes of suffering.

May we joyfully and lovingly accomplish compassionate activity for the sake of all sentient beings in all realms.

May the stream of Bodhicitta flow deep, strong and sweet, to quench the thirst of all beings.

May the fruit of merit ripen in our mind streams, nourishing all who are hungry.

May all who are homeless be sheltered, who are cold be warmed, who are sick be healed.

May all who are lonely be comforted, the helpless be raised up, the poor be satisfied in every way.

May our land be purified of hate and greed.

And may a song of freedom be heard throughout this and all nations. May we join as one life—which is our nature—and be unbound by hatred, greed and ignorance.

May there be peace and joy throughout the 3,000 myriads of universes! And may I myself bear in love, the suffering of all. Now and in the time to come.

December 9, 2011, revealed on Twitter.

From a series of tweets while at Palyul Ling Retreat Center in Upstate New York

To the victorious Guru Karma Kuchen I pray—for the sake of beings in these degenerate times, ascend the Lion Throne of Palyul fully endowed with every strength and virtue! May we who long for your blessing be satisfied!

In previous times you came to us as Karma Tashi to clear our ignorance, our attachment to ordinary confused appearance!

You again sat on the glorious Palyul throne to grant us the awakening to Primordial Buddha nature as the great display Karma Gyurmed, the dance of suchness, as it is!

Then you returned as Karma Thegchog Nyingpo, also known as Tsawei Lama by the peerless Guru, the Third Drubwang Pema Norbu Rinpoche.

You now have come again as Karma Kuchen, pure and stainless. Kye ho! Such are the many miracles of your display for the sake of beings. Now please abide steadfast upon the Lotus Throne of my heart. Rise this very moment, clear all obstacles to mighty Palyul, banish the enemies of the Heart Essence Nectar given to us by the second Buddha Padmasambava through the child Terton Migyur Dorje. Restore us all to original purity, clear recognition and perfect virtue!

May Palyul remain as the great unbroken refuge it is in the world now. Please establish the work of your predecessors and that of our Guru. Protect with mighty vigor the insurmountable accomplishment of our Guru Kyabje Pema Norbu, may nothing be wasted, and may all beings benefit! Live long! Strengthen the Throne of Palyul and remain in perfect health! Show your holy face as we hunger and thirst; and we need you now more than ever, in these darkening times we need your light, the sun of Palyul, Guru within my heart, grant your blessings!

August 2011

Dedication Prayer for Palyul and Kunzang Ödsal Palyul Changchub Chöling

From the land of Tibet came forth many
    lineages to the United States of America.
Among them is the Great Palyul Lineage.
From that Lineage came Kunzang Ödsal Palyul
    Changchub Chöling.
May noble Palyul and Kunzang Ödsal Palyul
    Changchub Chöling thrive until the end of time,
    and continue to flourish, prosper and benefit all
    sentient beings
May 24 hour prayer continue and bring boundless merit
    and blessings.

June 7, 2014

Dedication of Merit

By this effort, may all sentient beings
 be free of suffering.
May their minds be filled with the
 nectar of virtue.
In this way, may all causes resulting
 in suffering be extinguished,
And only the light of compassion
 shine throughout all realms.

1996

Photo: © Mannie Garcia

Images

Cover Jetsunma in prayer. Photo Mannie Garcia 2004.

p.10 Jetsunma's enthronement. Photo Ted Kurkowski 1988.

p.14 Thangka. White Umbrella. Photo Ani Sonam Schroeder 2018. Source: Jetsunma Ahkön Norbu Lhamo.

p.16 Thangka. 1000 armed Chenrezig. Photo Ani Aileen Williams 2005. Source: Kunzang Palyul Chöling, Poolesville, Maryland (MD).

p.19 Prayer vigil wall chart at Kunzang Palyul Chöling, Poolesville, MD. Photo Wib Middleton 1998.

p.20 Silhouette of Nun at Palyul Peace Park KPC MD. Photo Wib Middleton 2013.

p.22 Porch shot of Jetsunma with students, Palyul Ling Retreat Center, McDonough, New York (NY). Photo Ani Sonam Schroeder 2012.

p.24 Thangka. Close-up of Guru Rinpoche. Photo Ani Sonam Schroeder 2018. Source: Jetsunma Ahkön Norbu Lhamo.

p.27 Thangka. Four-armed Chenrezig. Photo Ani Aileen Williams 2007. Source: Kunzang Palyul Chöling, Poolesville, MD.

p.28 Composite photo of Jetsunma's ordained students. Graphic design Ashby North 2015.

p.30 Jetsunma on throne meeting student. Photo Ani Dawa Dellamulla 2004.

p.34 Shakyamuni Buddha Altar, Kunzang Palyul Chöling, Poolesville, MD. Photo Wib Middleton 2006.

p.36 Thangka. Close-up of Vajrasattva. Photo Ani Aileen Williams 1994. Source: Tibetan Meditation Center, Frederick, MD.

p.38   Thangka. Green Tara. Photo Ani Sonam Schroeder 2018. Source: Jetsunma Ahkön Norbu Lhamo.

p.42   Thangka. Wheel of Life. Photo Wib Middleton 1987. Source: Kunzang Palyul Chöling, Poolesville, MD.

p.52   Thangka. Princess Lhacham Mandarava. Photo Ani Sonam Schroeder. Source: Jetsunma Ahkön Norbu Lhamo.

p.54   Thangka. Close-up of Yeshe Tsogyal. Photo Ani Sonam Schroeder 2018. Source: Jetsunma Ahkön Norbu Lhamo.

p.56   HH Penor Norbu Rinpoche on throne at KPC. Photo Mannie Garcia 2003.

p.58   Jetsunma walking with Ani Sonam Schroeder. Photo Ani Dawa Dellamulla 2013.

p.60   HH Penor Norbu Rinpoche on throne at Palyul Ling Retreat Center, McDonough, NY. Photo Wib Middleton 1997.

p.62   The Yangsi (reincarnation) of HH Penor Norbu Rinpoche. Photographer unknown, Palyul, Tibet 2017.

p.64   Thangka. Amitaba. Photo Ani Aileen 2007. Source: Kunzang Palyul Chöling, Poolesville, MD.

p.67   Laminate of Thangka. Amitaba and entourage. Photo Ani Aileen Williams 1991. Source: Kunzang Palyul Chöling, Poolesville, MD.

p.68   The Famous Amitaba Stupa in Sedona, Arizona built by Jetsunma. Photo Wib Middleton 2018.

p.70   HH Karma Kuchen. Photo Mannie Garcia 2003.

p.72   Thangka. Close-up of Princess Lhacham Mandarava. Photo Ani Sonam Schroeder. Source: Jetsunma Ahkön Norbu Lhamo.

p.74   HH Karma Kuchen. Photo Ani Sonam Schroeder 2011.

p.76 Long Life Puja for HH Penor Norbu Rinpoche at the Golden Temple, Namdroling, India. Photo Palyul Namdroling, Losar 2009.

p.79 Jetsunma praying. Photo Mannie Garcia 2004.

p.88 Jetsunma at Dakini Valley near Young, Arizona. Photo Ani Sonam Schroeder 2014.

Glossary

Amitabha: Buddha Amitabha is one of the Buddhas of the five Buddha families embodying the Dharmakaya (enlightenment principle) in varying displays. Buddha Amitabha is red in color and represents mirror-like wisdom. (See also 'Amoghasiddhi','Enlightenment','Five Dhyani Buddhas','Ratnasambhava' and 'Vairocana' in this Glossary.)

Amoghasiddhi: Buddha Amoghasiddhi is one of the Buddhas of the five Buddha families embodying the Dharmakaya (enlightenment principle) in varying displays. Buddha Amoghasiddhi is green in color and represents the wisdom of the perfection of practice. (See also 'Amitabha', 'Enlightenment', 'Five Dhyani Buddhas', 'Ratnasambhava' and 'Vairocana' in this Glossary.)

Bodhicitta: The mind of enlightenment that encompasses wisdom and compassion.

Buddha: The historical founder of Buddhism, Shakyamuni. Also, one who is completely awake to the true nature of reality.

Buddhahood: One who is a Buddha is also referred to as one who has attained 'Buddhahood.'

Dakini: The wisdom aspect in female form. A Dakini can appear in human form including as a consort, as a meditational deity and as a protector of the Dharma.

Dharma: The pure path taught by the Buddha that leads one out of suffering into the awakened state of enlightenment. Dharma is the underlying meaning of the Buddha's teachings; the truth upon which all Buddhist practices, scriptures and philosophy are based.

Dharmakaya: The primordial limitless form of the Buddha.

Dharmadhatu: The 'realm of phenomena'; the suchness of the resting mind in which emptiness and dependent origination are inseparable.

Enlightenment: The cessation of suffering reached when the qualities of compassion and wisdom are perfected and all non-virtue has been extinguished from one's mind.

Five Dhyani Buddhas: The five wisdom Buddha families embodying the Dharmakaya (enlightenment principle) in varying displays. They are Buddha Vairocana, Amoghasiddhi, Amitabha, Ratnasambhava and Akshobya (See also 'Amitabha', 'Amoghasiddhi', Enlightenment' 'Dharmakaya', and 'Ratnasambhava' and 'Vairocana' in this Glossary.)

Genyenma Ahkön Lhamo: A remarkable female master of the 17th century who lived close to the first Palyul Monastery where she attracted many students, particularly nuns. She was the sister of Vidyadhara Kunzang Sherab (the first throneholder of the Palyul lineage). Like her brother she received direct teachings from Tertön Migyur Dorje. (See also 'Tertön Migyur Dorjé' and 'Rigdzin Kunzang Sherab' in this Glossary.)

Guru: One's spiritual teacher.

His Holiness Dudjom Rinpoche: One of Tibet's most outstanding meditation masters, poets and scholars (1904-1987) who was recognized as an incarnation of Tertön Dudjom Lingpa. His Holiness wrote the complete history of the Nyingma lineage, and was the first appointed head of the Nyingma lineage in the 20th century. He was instrumental in establishing the Nyingma School of Vajrayana Buddhism in the West.

His Holiness Karma Kuchen (Karma Tashi - Karma Gyurmed – Karma Thegchog Nyingpo): (1970-): The extraordinary fourteenth throne holder of the Palyul lineage in the Nyingma School of Vajrayana Buddhism. His Holiness is the fifth incarnation of Karma Kuchen Rinpoche.

His Holiness Kusum Lingpa: A renowned master, Nyingma lineage holder and Tertön, also known as Orgyen Kusum Lingpa and Padma Tumdrak Duddul Dorje Rolpatsal (1934-2009). He gave teachings and empowerments at KPC in 1994. At this time he recognized Jetsunma as an emanation of White Tara, and of Princess Lhacham Mandarava, the Indian consort of Padmasambhava.

His Holiness Ngawang Tenzin: The Dorje Lopon (Master of Ritual) of Bhutan in 2004, who visited KPC in that same year to offer teachings and empowerments. His Holiness composed a long-life prayer for Jetsunma at that time and confirmed her as an incarnation of Mandarava.

His Holiness Penor Rinpoche (Third Drubwang): The sublime thirteenth throne holder of the Palyul lineage in the Nyingma School of Vajrayana Buddhism and the third incarnation of Drubwang Pema Norbu Rinpoche. His Holiness recognized Jetsunma as a reincarnation of Genyenma Ahkön Lhamo, and guided Jetsunma in the establishment of Kunzang Palyul Chöling. (See 'Genyenma Ahkön Lhamo' in this Glossary.)

Kunzang Palyul Chöling: The name of the Buddhist Temple in the Nyingma-Palyul lineage of Vajrayana Buddhism established by Jetsunma Ahkön Norbu Lhamo under the guidance of His Holiness Penor Norbu Rinpoche in the USA. The name Kunzang Palyul Chöling is often shortened to the acronym, 'KPC'. The full name of KPC is Kunzang Ödsal Palyul Changchub Chöling.

Kyabje: An honorific title reserved for respected and accomplished masters in the Vajrayana tradition. Kyabje translates as Lord of Refuge and is sometimes rendered in English as His Holiness.

Lion Throne: The seat of Buddha Shakyamuni, in this instance referring to the throne of the Buddhist Master, His Holiness Karma Kuchen Rinpoche, ascending to the Palyul lineage throne as the 14th throne holder.

Lotus Lord: Padmasambhava (otherwise known as Guru Rinpoche) who, through his extraordinary qualities and realization, ensured the establishment of Buddhism in Tibet in the 8th century. In the Nyingma School of Vajrayana Buddhism he is considered to be the condensed essence of all the Buddhas.

Lotus Posture: The ideal cross-legged seated posture for meditation in which the feet are placed on the opposing thighs. In Sanskrit this posture is called Padmasana.

Lotus Throne: The Lotus throne is the seat of the Buddha. It can also refer to the heart center, considered to be the seat of the mind in Vajrayana Buddhism.

Mala: A Buddhist rosary, commonly made up of 108 beads. A mala is a support for counting, for instance in mantra recitation and prostrations.

Mandala: A physical or visual display of enlightened activity.

Nirmanakaya: The display of enlightenment, commonly in human form.

Om Mani Pedme Hung: The mantra of the Buddha of Compassion, Avalokiteshvara (Chenrezig) in Sambhogakaya form. (See also 'Sambhogakaya' in this Glossary.)

Om Tare Tuttare Ture So Ha: The mantra of Tara, the Sambhogakaya Buddha, in female form. (See also 'Sambhogakaya' in this Glossary.)

Padmasambhava: See 'Lotus Lord' in this Glossary.

Palyul: One of six Nyingma lineages in Vajrayana Buddhism in Tibet. The Palyul lineage was established in 1665 by the King of Dege, Lhachen Jampa Phuntsog, and Trichen Sangye Tanpa in Eastern Tibet.

Ratnasambhava: Buddha Ratnasambhava is one of the Buddhas of the five Buddha families that embodies the Dharmakaya (enlightenment principle) in varying displays. Buddha Ratnasambhava is gold or yellow in color, and represents the wisdom of equanimity. (See also 'Amitabha', 'Amoghasiddhi', 'Enlightenment', 'Five Dhyani Buddhas', 'Ratnasambhava' and 'Vairocana' in this Glossary.)

Rigdzin Kunzang Sherab: The first throne holder and Abbot of Palyul monastery in Tibet, also referred to as Vidyadhara Kunzang Sherab. Vidyadhara Kunzang Sherab was one of the main disciples of Tertön Migyur Dorjé, and the first dharma keeper of the Nam Chö cycle of teachings. (See also 'Tertön Migyur Dorjé' in this Glossary.)

Sambhogakaya: The clear light or bliss form of the Buddha.

Samsara: The endless round of death and rebirth, characterized by impermanence, cause and effect, suffering, and ignorance of true reality.

Sangha: The community of Buddhist monks and nuns; may also refer to lay practitioners.

Ship to Liberation: The Ship to Liberation is the Buddhist path.

Tara: A Sambhogakaya form of the Buddha in female form. (See also 'Sambhogakaya' in this Glossary.)

Tathagatas: A Sanskrit and Pali word referring to the Buddha (in this case Buddhas plural) that translates in English as "one who has thus gone".

Tertön Migyur Dorje: Tertön Migyur Dorje (1645-1667) revealed the Nam Chö (Sky Space Treasure) cycle of termas. The Nam Chö cycle is a core cycle of teachings in the Palyul lineage.

Three Precious Jewels: The Buddha, the Dharma (Buddhist teachings) and the Sangha (the community of practitioners). (See also 'Sangha' in this Glossary.)

Three thousand myriads of universes: Referring indicatively to the countless number of universes in Vajrayana cosmology.

Vairocana: The primordial wisdom Buddha in Dharmakaya form of the five Buddha families. Vairocana is white in color, denoting the blending of all colors and therefore the sum of all the qualities of all the Dhyani Buddhas. (See also 'Amitabha','Amoghasiddhi','Enlightenment','Five Dhyani Buddhas' and 'Ratnasambhava' in this Glossary.)

Vajrasattva: A Sambhogakaya form of the Buddha associated with purification. (See also 'Sambhogakaya' in this Glossary.)

Vajrayana: Of the three vehicles of Buddhism, the one that also contains the other vehicles—Theravada and Mahayana—within it. Vajrayana, otherwise known as the "Diamond Vehicle," is practiced mostly by Buddhists following the Tibetan, Mongolian and Himalayan forms of Buddhism.

Venerable Gyaltrul Rinpoche: Venerable Gyaltrul Rinpoche (1925-), in his previous incarnation, was Vidyadhara Kunzang Sherab, the first throne holder and Abbot of the Palyul lineage, and brother of Jetsunma's previous incarnation (Genyenma Ahkön Lhamo). Venerable Gyaltrul Rinpoche moved to the USA in 1972 following a request by HH the Dalai Lama and HH Dudjom Rinpoche. Venerable Gyaltrul Rinpoche has significantly helped KPC and Jetsunma, particularly during its establishment phase. (See 'Rigdzin Kunzang Sherab' in this Glossary.)

Venerable Khenpo Palden Sherab: Nyingma master (1938-2010) who, along with his brother, Venerable Khenpo Tsewang Dongyal, were among the first wave of Nyingma teachers in the USA, arriving in 1980. Venerable Khenpo Palden Sherab, through the request of HH Dudjom Rinpoche, was also instrumental in recovering thousands of texts and commentaries. Khenpo Palden Sherab and his brother were also among the earliest teachers at KPC, first visiting in 1986 to give teachings.

Venerable Khenpo Tsewang Dongyal: (1950-) See above. Khenpo, with his brother, established Padmasambhava Buddhist Centers, and has extensively published on the Dharma for English language speakers, including poetry on the life of Padmasambhava (Guru Rinpoche).

About Jetsunma Ahkön Norbu Lhamo

From an early age, Jetsunma Ahkön Norbu Lhamo has devoted herself to meditation and the alleviation of suffering in the world. With confirmation from two highly revered Tibetan Buddhist masters, His Holiness Dilgo Khyentse Rinpoche and Dzongnang Rinpoche, His Holiness Penor Rinpoche, 11th throneholder of the Palyul Lineage in the Nyingma tradition, recognized Jetsunma as a reincarnation of the 17th century yogini Genyenma Ahkön Lhamo. The first Ahkön Lhamo was the sister of Rigdzin Kunzang Sherab, the founder and first Throneholder of Palyul.

Subsequently, His Holiness Kusum Lingpa recognized Jetsunma as an emanation of Princess Lhacham Mandarava, the Indian consort of Padmasambhava (also known as Guru Rinpoche, or Precious Teacher), the Indian scholar who stabilized Buddhism in Tibet. Jetsunma is the first Western woman to have been officially recognized and enthroned as a Tulku, an enlightened being who reincarnates in whatever form necessary to benefit sentient beings.

In 1985, Jetsunma established Kunzang Palyul Chöling (KPC) at the request of His Holiness Penor Rinpoche. When His Holiness returned to America in 1988, he offered the Rinchen Terdzöd, the great treasury of revealed teachings (terma) for the first time in the United States at KPC. At that time, His Holiness consecrated the first of the 19 Stupas that currently stand on the property. Teachings are continually offered at KPC where there is a community of 30+ monks and nuns as well as many lay practitioners. With the additional guidance of a resident Khenpo, students continue their Dharma study and learn how to conduct ritual practices in the Palyul tradition. In 2015, the KPC Sangha celebrated its 30th year of prayer around the clock, upholding a commitment to maintain continuous prayer until there is no more suffering. Visitors come to KPC to meditate and pray day and night.

With innate compassion and wisdom, and drawing on her experiences as a Western woman, Jetsunma makes even the most profound Buddhist teachings accessible. Her teachings, often infused with humor, reach a broad audience, including long-time Buddhist practitioners as well as people simply wanting to live with kindness and generosity. Jetsunma encourages each of us to create a world of compassion, by contemplating the suffering of others and taking action to bring about change.